Step by Step Book for Loom Bead Weaving Mastery
Unlock Your Creativity with Easy to Follow

Raymond A Theodore

Table of Contents

Chapter One — 3
    Beading Making on a Bead Loom — 3
    Varieties of Bead Looms — 3

Chapter Two — 4
    How to Use a Bead Loom: A Primer on Jewelry Making — 4
    Supplies — 5
    1. Set up the Loom — 5

Chapter Three — 8
    2. Commence Weaving — 8

Chapter Four — 14
    3. Construct the Plan — 14
    4. Remove the Work From the Loom — 16

Chapter Five — 34
    Simple Bead Weaving Loom and Bracelet Introduction — 34
    Step 1: Materials for the Loom and Bracelet — 37
    Components of Beaded Bracelet — 39
    Bracelet Design — 40
    Step 2: Establishing the Loom and Threads — 40

Chapter Six — 43
    Step 3: Commence Beading on the Loom — 43
    Step 4: Complete the Beaded Bracelet on the Loom — 46
    Avoid These Common Beginning Beading Mistakes — 49
    Beadwork With Excessive Thread — 50
    Incorrect Beading Thread Tension — 51
    Separating Beading Thread — 51
    Fear of Trying New Beadwork Stitches — 52

Chapter One

Beading Making on a Bead Loom

A bead loom is a device used to weave together beads. Beading looms all have the same fundamental construction, in which weaving is accomplished by placing the weft threads (threads that run from side to side) over and under the fixed warp threads (up and down threads). The weft threads, which hold your beads, are weaved between the warp threads, which are kept in place by tension. The length and quantity of your warp threads will define the length and breadth of your completed product.

Varieties of Bead Looms

Although all bead looms have the same fundamental design, there are variations across models. A kit like as the BeadSmith Bead Loom Kit for Beginners would be an excellent option for beginners. It is a conventionally constructed bead loom that includes needles, threads, and beads to get you started. The Beadalon Jewel Loom is another option; its small size makes it ideal for travel. It also features notches to appropriately separate your warp threads. Many of our Exclusive Beadaholique Loom Bracelet Jewelry Kits contain a Jewel Loom.

Consider the Ricks Beading Loom for a new experience. This style leaves just two threads protruding from either end, as opposed to the many warp threads left by conventional looms. Deb Moffett-The Hall's Endless Loom goes much farther and left no warp ends to tie up.

Grab a Wrapit Loom from Rainbow Loom to produce bracelets in the ladder-wrap design.

Chapter Two

How to Use a Bead Loom: A Primer on Jewelry Making

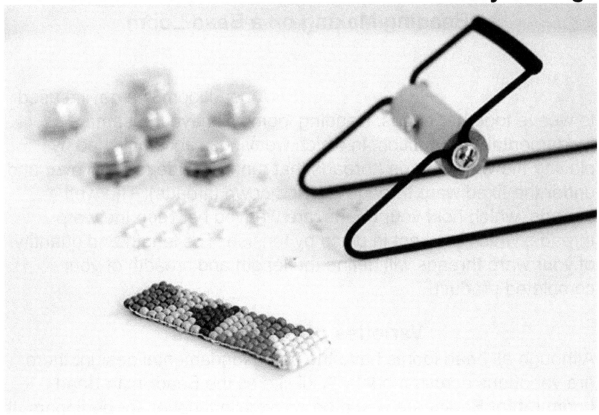

What You Will Be Making

Tribal motifs are a summer must-have for this decade. Navajo, Ganado, and Chinle designs are reinterpreted annually with new colors, methods, and applications. Printing and beading are recurrent techniques for investigating the shapes used commonly in fashion, accessories, and interiors.

If you've ever attempted beading with simply a needle and thread, you know that it's a lengthy process. Incorporating pattern into a design requires a process that is hard, time-consuming, and off-putting to most.

Bring out the bead loom. This sort of loom has been utilized in both traditional and contemporary beadwork, and it makes beadwork considerably quicker and simpler, with a much greater scope for pattern creation. Even if you're a novice, you can create patterns that are larger and of higher quality than by hand! Read on to learn how.

Supplies

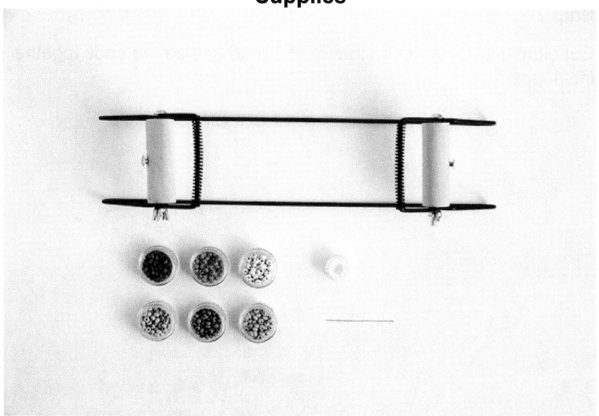

- Bead Loom
- Beads of Seed
- The Bead Needle
- Thread
- Scissors

1. Set up the Loom

Step 1

First, we must establish the warp strands (the ones that are attached to the loom). Determine the width of the design. I've decided to make a strip seven beads wide (if you want to build triangle forms, always choose an odd number so you obtain a "one bead" point in the center). Add one to the number of beads to get the number of warp threads required.

Step 2

Cut eight one-meter-long strands of thread and tie the ends together into loops.

Step 3

Hook the loops onto the wooden barrels of the loom and roll to produce tension by tightening the threads. Separate the threads into distinct gaps between the barrels on the coil. A crochet hook is an extremely useful tool for separating threads.

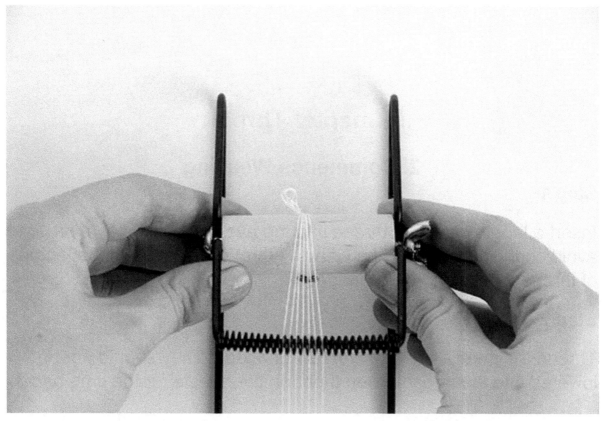

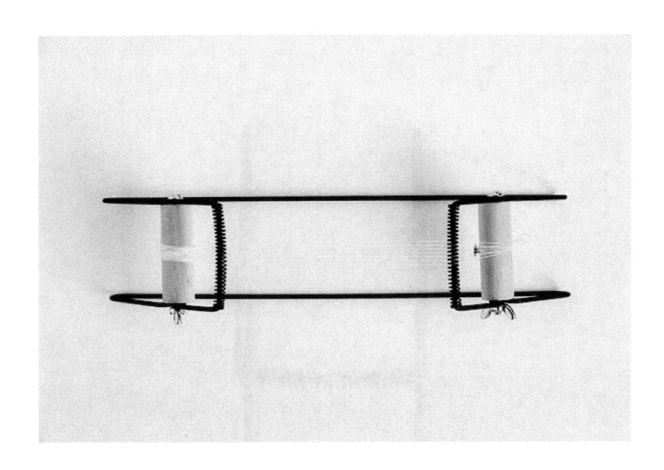

Chapter Three

2. Commence Weaving

Step 1

Insert a lengthy piece of thread into the eye of the needle. In order to avoid changing the weft (the weaving thread) too often, cut a length of thread that is long yet manageable.

Step 2

Thread the needle with the first row of beads. They should not be lowered into the thread. Keep them on the needle for the time being.

Step 3

Position the needle on top of the warp threads and place each bead between two warp threads.

Use your finger to keep the beads in place as you thread the needle through them. Leave a lengthy thread tail dangling from the bead in front.

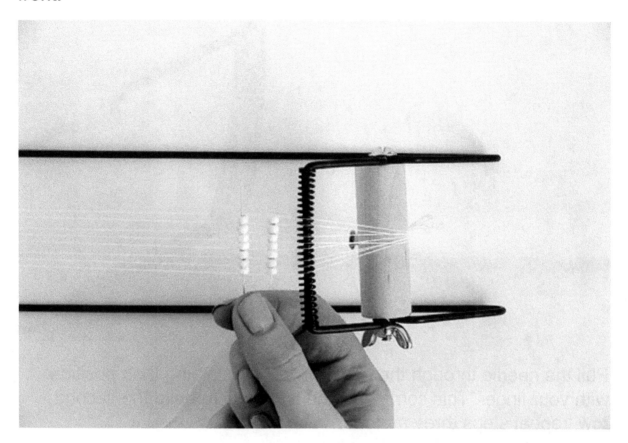

Step 4

Reverse the needle and thread it back through the beads. This time, ensure that the needle passes under each warp thread as you thread it through the bead holes.

Pull the needle through the beads while maintaining their position with your finger. This completes the first row! To build the second row, repeat steps three and four.

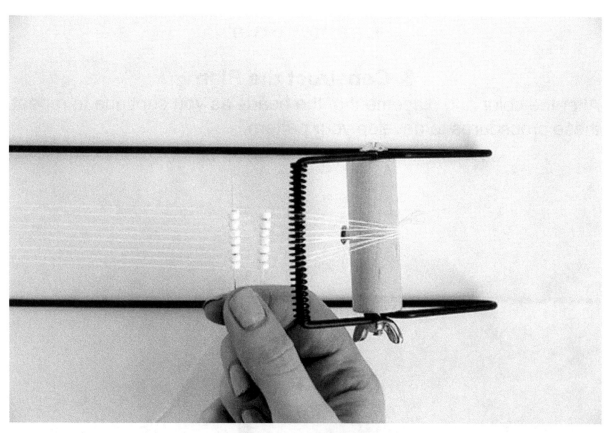
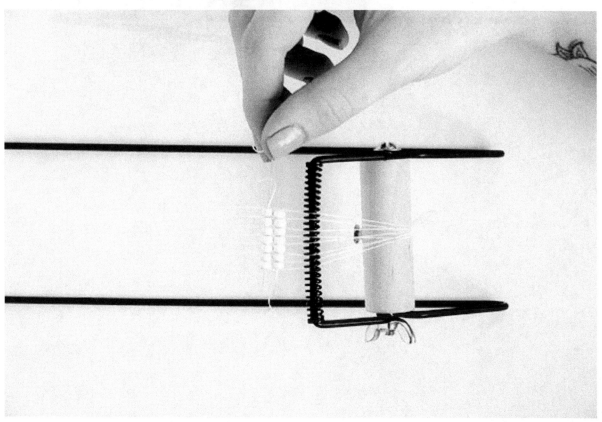

Chapter Four

3. Construct the Plan

Alter the color and placement of the beads as you continue to repeat these procedures to develop your pattern.

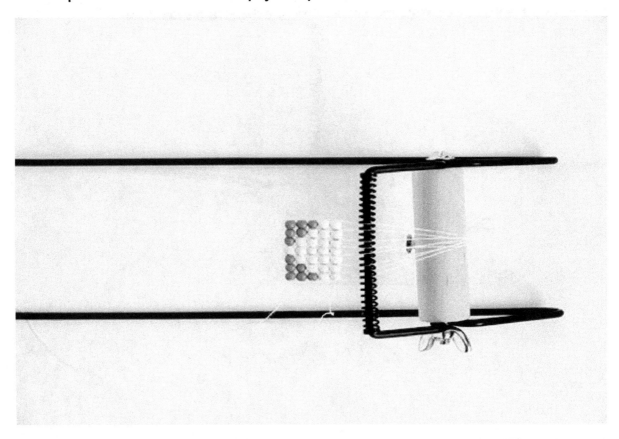

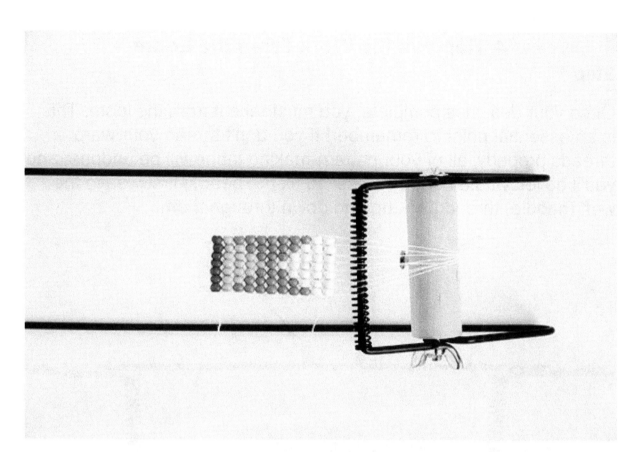
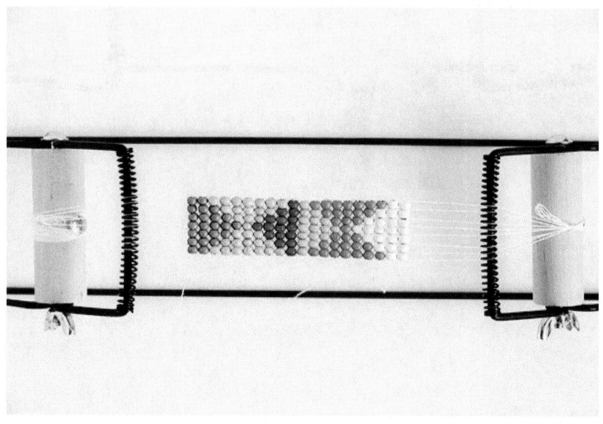

4. Remove the Work From the Loom

Step 1

Once your design is complete, you must take it from the loom. This is an essential point to remember! If you don't thread your warp threads properly, all of your pattern-making labor will be undone, and you'll be left with a beaded mess! To fix the beads, first weave the weft (needle) thread back up and down through them.

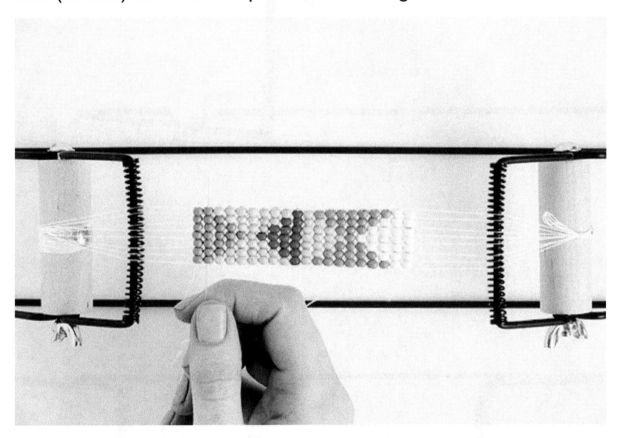

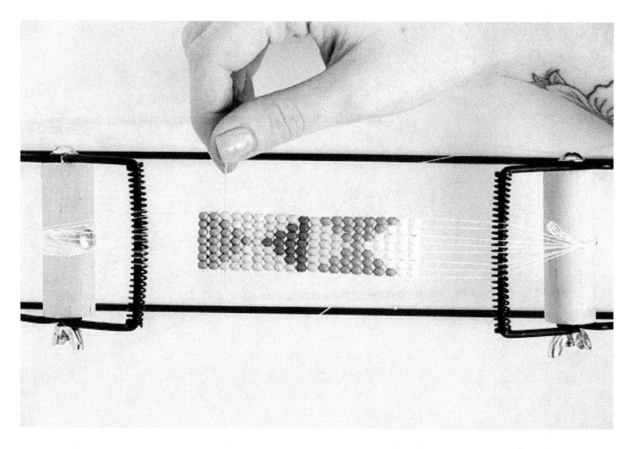

After stringing many rows, trim the extra in the center of a row. This conceals the work's central theme.

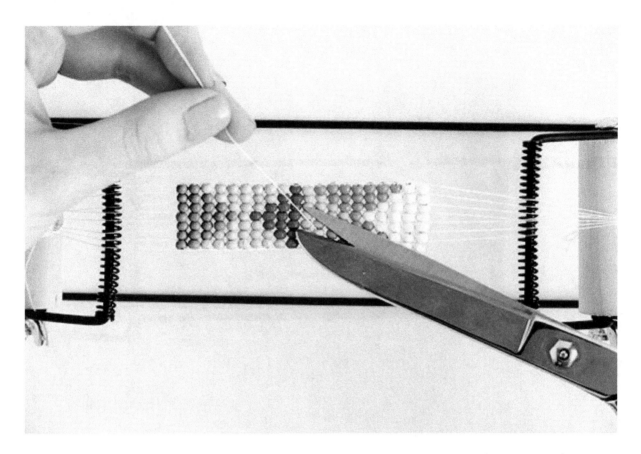

Repeat with the thread "tail" we left at the beginning of the item.

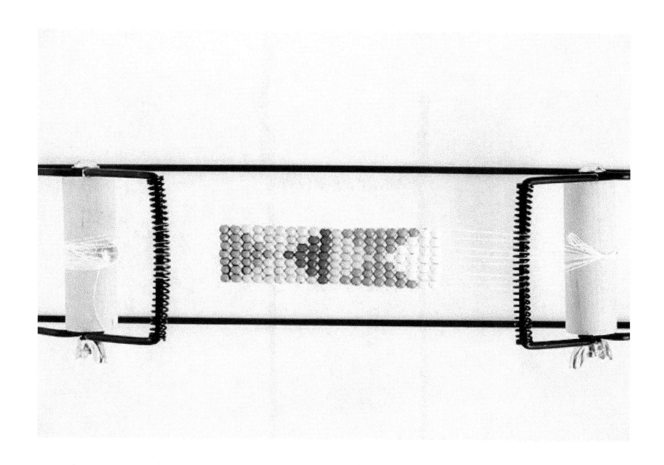

Step 2

Beginning at any end of the loom, loosen the threads by unwinding the barrel. Cut the thread on the far right to a length of about 15 centimeters or 6 inches.

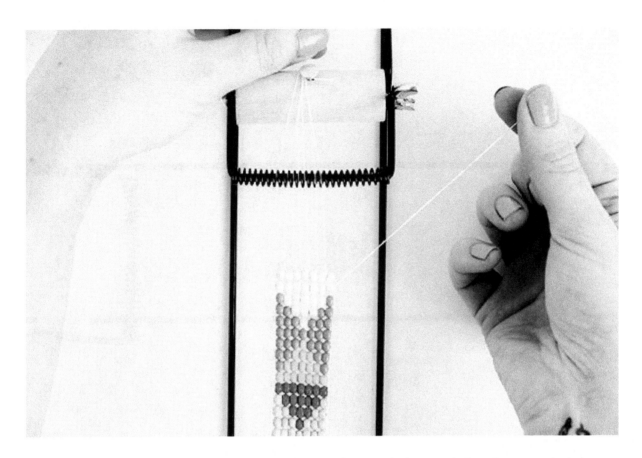

Restriction the remaining warp threads and thread the loose right thread onto a needle.

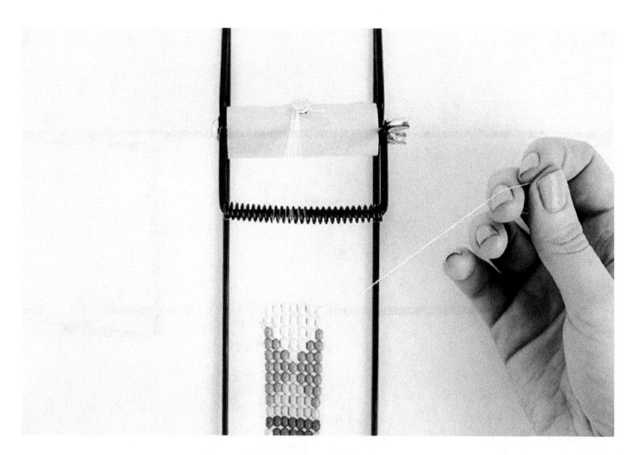

Beginning with the first two beads of the first row and the first two beads of the second row, weave this thread into the pattern.

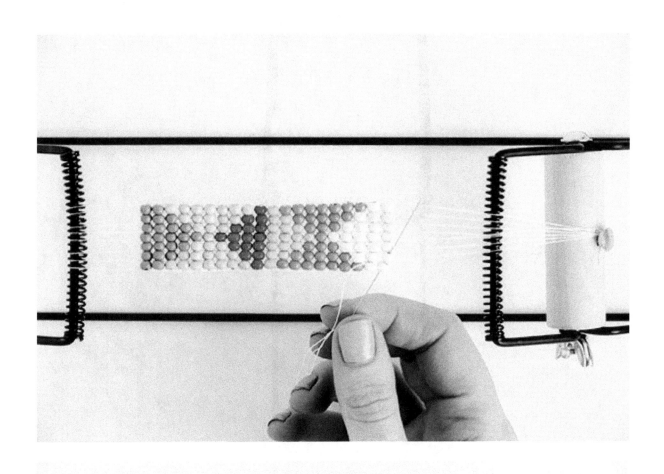
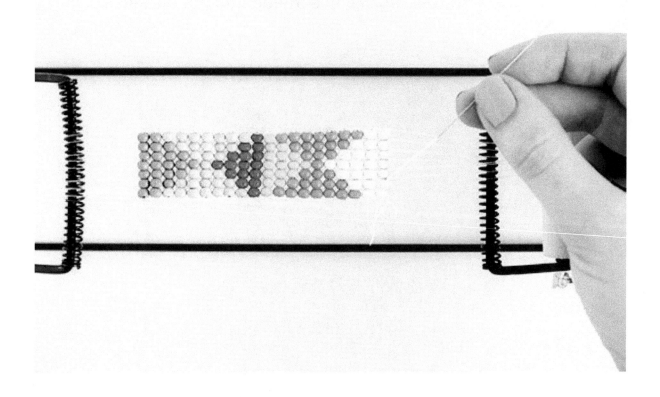

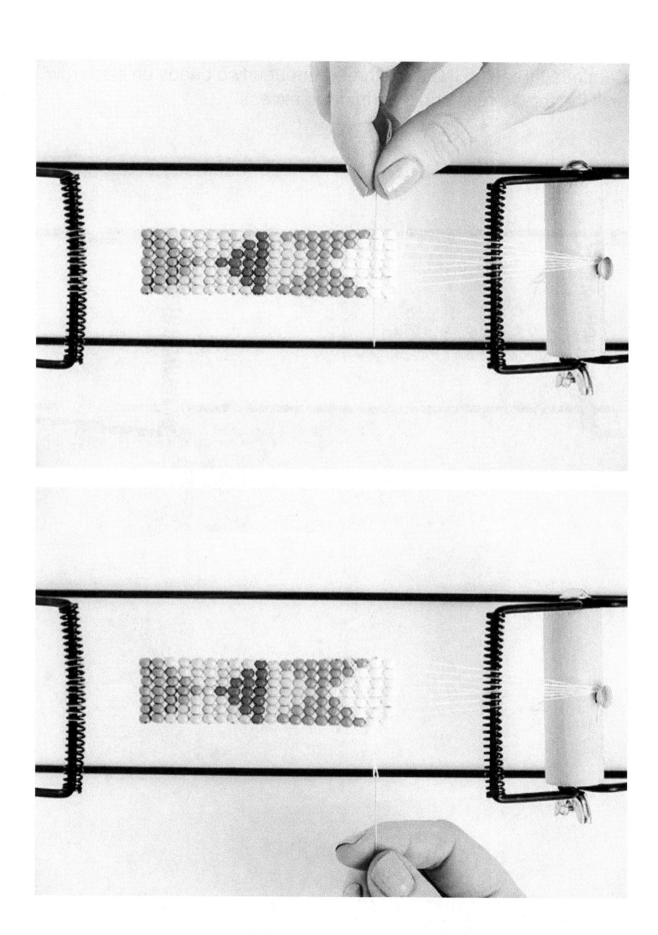

Continue threading the warp thread through two beads on each row until the thread runs out, then trim the excess.

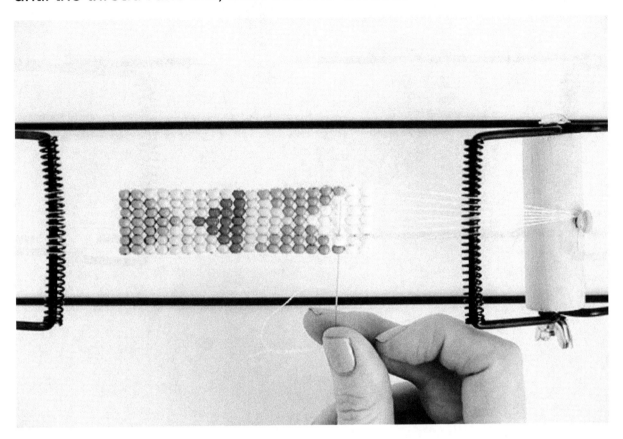

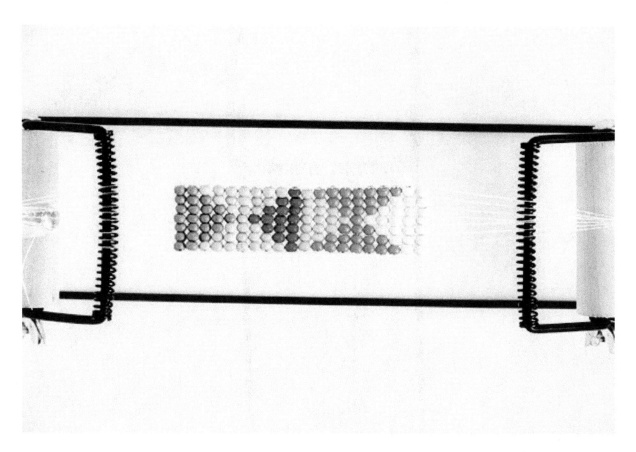

Step 3

Remove the next warp thread from the loom in the exact same manner as previously.

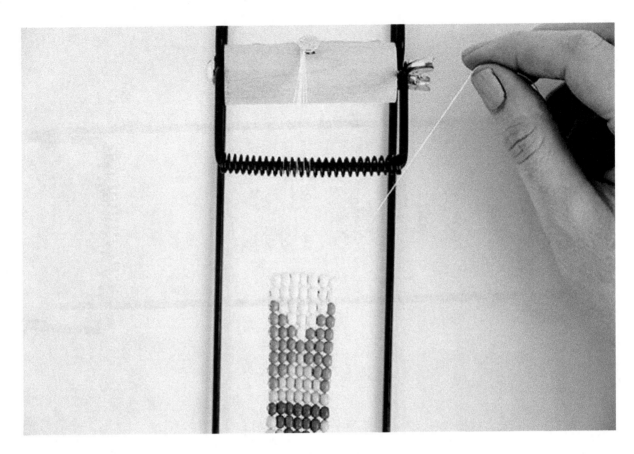

Begin to weave this into the work. This time, you will go through the second and third beads from each row's end.

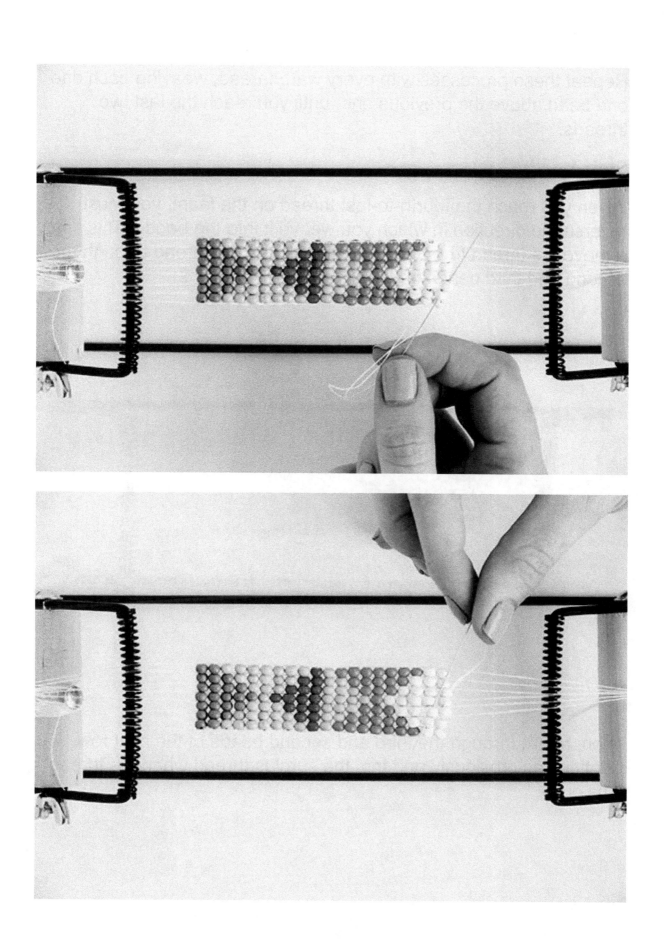

Repeat these processes with every warp thread, weaving each one one bead above the previous one, until you reach the last two threads.

Step 4

When you reach the fourth-to-last thread on the loom, you must reverse the direction in which you weave it into the beads. This time, remove the thread from the loom and weave the thread through the second and third beads on the other side.

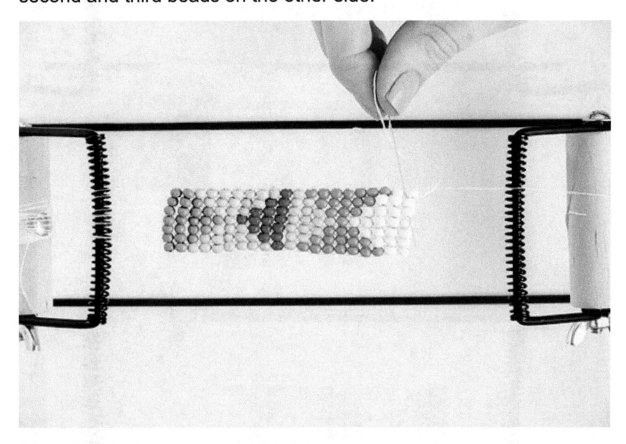

Then, return through the third and second beads of the next row. Continue as previously and trim the surplus thread when the thread runs out.

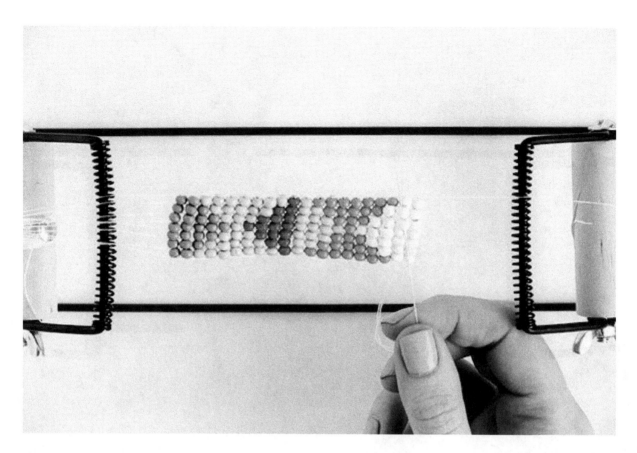

Step 5

When you reach the last warp thread, remove the loom and thread the warp through the first and second beads of each row while holding the work in your hand. As soon as you reach the end of the thread, trim the extra.

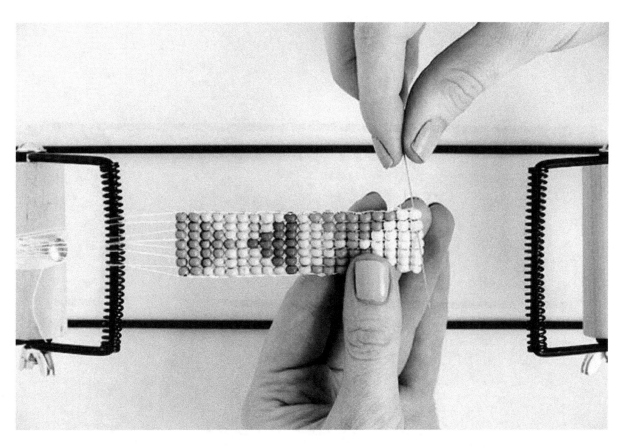
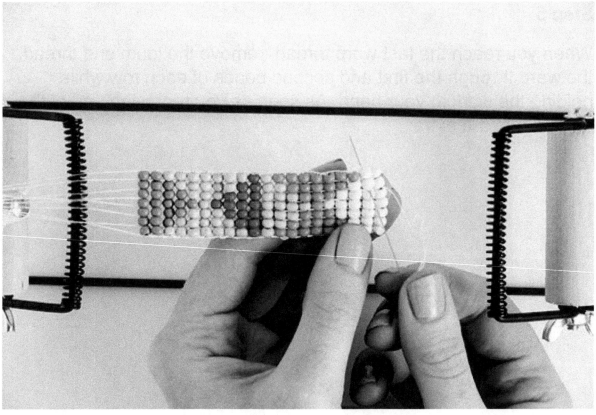

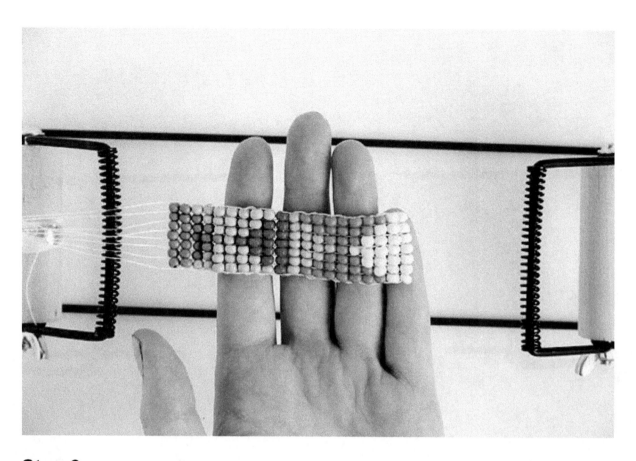

Step 6

Repeat steps 2 through 5 on the other side of the loom.

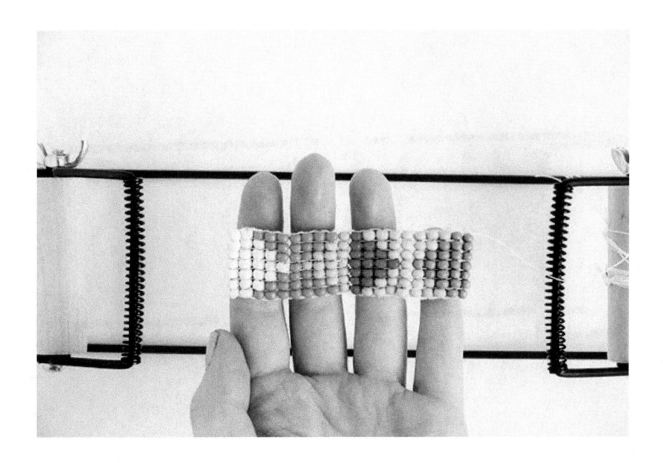

Once you've completed threading the last warp thread, your fabric is sturdy and ready for use!

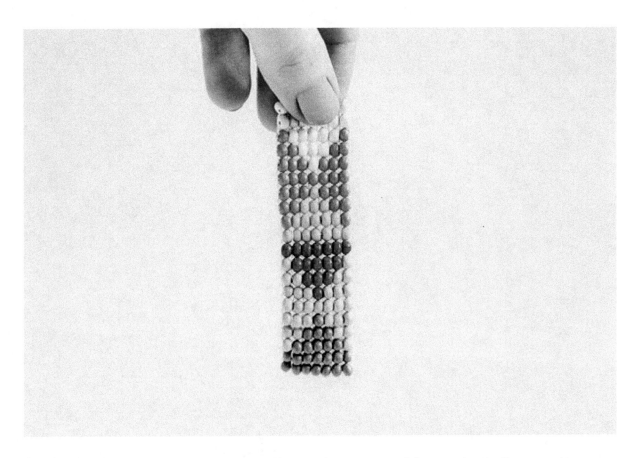

This lesson addressed threading a loom, making a beading pattern and shape, and removing beaded work from a loom. Be remember to return to Tuts+ for upcoming lessons on turning your beaded creations into functional objects.

Chapter Five

Simple Bead Weaving Loom and Bracelet Introduction

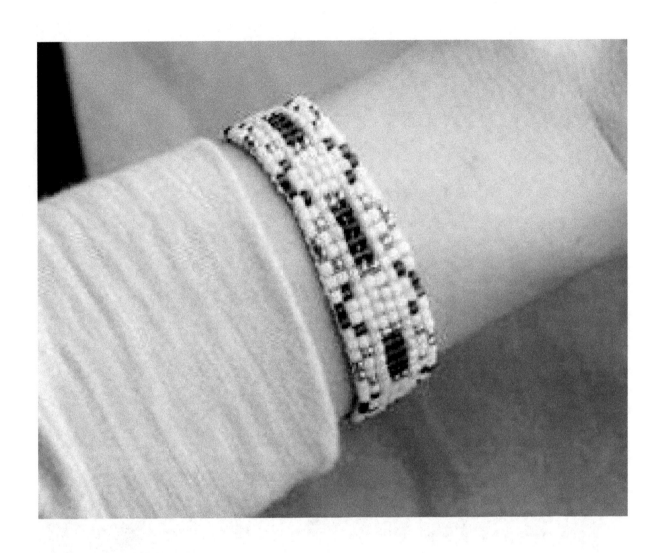

In this Book, I will demonstrate how to construct a small bead-weaving loom using wood scraps and household debris. And I'll walk you through the steps of crafting a really one-of-a-kind beaded bracelet. I created two that differ in style. My favorite is the one that does not have a suede backing. In terms of design, there are an infinite number of possibilities. Let's get started!

Step 1: Materials for the Loom and Bracelet

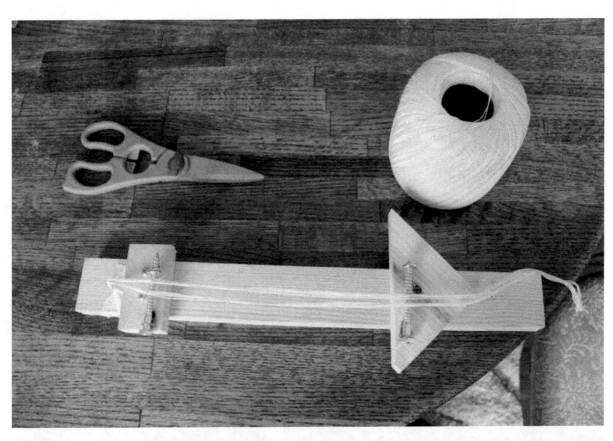
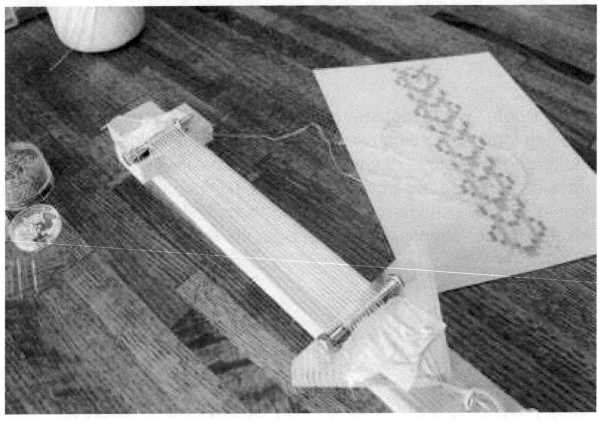

Materials for Weaving

1. a 12-inch-long piece of scrap wood.

2. two little pieces of wood to connect to the top of the main board (as you can see, I used scraps)

3. Two bolts, around the width of your board, are required.

4. Six eye-rings or eye-bolts and a few screws are required to connect little wood pieces to a board.

Components of Beaded Bracelet

1. An assortment of beads; I used tiny seed beads

2. Thread - I suggest bead weaving thread - I used Beadalon WildFire 0.006in or 0.15mm

• If you do not have bead weaving thread, you may substitute embroidery thread.

- Because embroidery thread is excessively thick, you will need to separate it and only use a few strands.

3. Beading Needles - I purchased a package of sizes 10-13, and they performed well.

4. Scissors with round-nose pliers, or a jewelry multi-tool with pliers

5. Glue - I used fabric glue, although bead weaving glue is available on Amazon

6. Optional: leather or suede

7. bracelet clasps

8. Optional: you may wish to get a threading tool, since it is really hard to thread these small needles.

Bracelet Design

Two bracelets were created for this Book. Both patterns are accessible to you here. You are free to create your own pattern on this website if you so like. The book is great since you can create a design in a matter of minutes, or even upload a picture, and it will turn it into a cross-stitch pattern suitable for this bead weaving activity.

Step 2: Establishing the Loom and Threads

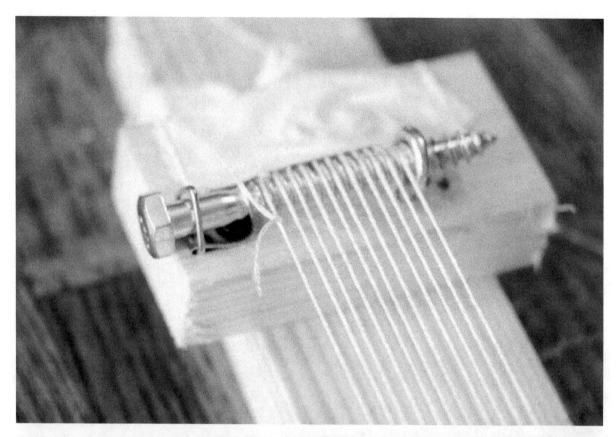
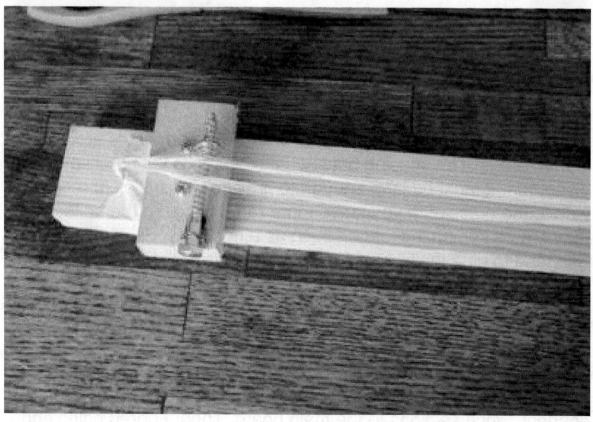

I created a pretty basic loom. If you already have a loom, please disregard the following two paragraphs. I climbed over various stuff in my garage to collect wood scraps, nuts, and screws for my loom and supplies. My lengthy piece of wood is about 16 inches long and two inches broad. Ideal would be if you had a broader piece of wood than what I used. Some individuals want a portion that is around six inches broad. The spacing between the two bolts is entirely at your discretion. It must be long enough to provide you sufficient room to weave the bracelet. If you leave more room between the bolts, you may create something longer, such as a necklace. Essentially, you will need to glue the two smaller wood pieces to the larger component. I left eight inches of space between the two linked pieces of wood on my loom.

The two little pieces were drilled into the main board. If you notice that I've connected oddly shaped parts, it's because that's all I had available. If I ever create a truly excellent loom in the future, I will connect 1 inch sections to the main board. Then, I bored holes and added two eye-bolts so the huge bolt could be inserted (see image for closeup). In addition, the screw's ridges serve as a great retainer and divider for the thread. Lastly, I placed eyebolts about an inch behind the joined top wood pieces. These are put there so that the thread's beginning and end may be linked to anything. If you're utilizing a simple arrangement like this, you should also have some duct tape on hand in case you need to secure the threads.

I constructed two bracelets and supplied two design templates. The bigger (wider) bracelet used eleven threads, while the smaller bracelet utilized nine. Once you have determined what you want to produce, you may cut the appropriate amount of threads, also known as warp threads. Tie a knot at the end, if required around the eye bolt, to fasten the top portion to the weaving loom. Some individuals just tie a loop knot over the eye-bolt. Then, determine the thread positioning by hand in order to split the parts and tie the other end to the second eye-bolt. Once you've mastered this with this simple loom, just ensure that the threads are pulled tightly. It will make beading much simpler. Attaching the top portion to the eye-bolt and then pulling it tight, I wrapped the lower end around the bottom eye-bolt and used duct tape to produce the tight threads. I didn't need to tie a knot completely. I just required that it be tight and secure. Do whatever serves you best. Then, I gently spaced the threads so that they lined up with the bolt's ridges and were ready for use.

Next, thread the needle with a few feet of the bead weaving thread. Due of the tiny needle apertures, I found this step to be a little challenging. However, I was able to thread it finally.

Chapter Six

Step 3: Commence Beading on the Loom

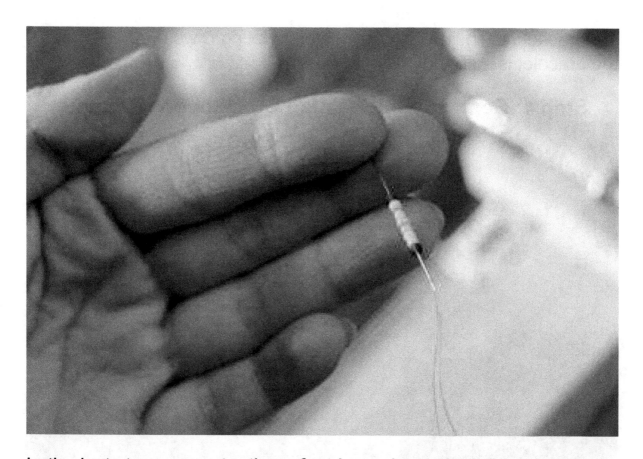

In the last step, you cut a three-foot-long piece of thread. You have threaded the needle and must now tie a knot close to where you will begin beading (left-side warp thread). Be cautious to allow four to six inches of extra thread while tying this knot. When you're through stringing beads, you'll deal with the remaining thread. For me, I just tie the knot and duct tape the spare thread strand to the other threads.

Examine the design to determine what color beads are required. Then, using the needle, pick up the beads and thread them onto the thread and then below the warp threads. Once the beads are positioned between the warp threads, you push them up with one hand and pass the needle through them again with the other (this time above the warp threads). This is difficult to describe yet incredibly simple to do. Here is a really little video tutorial that I created for you. I will upload more videos covering further phases in the future. Currently, I have several photographs to assist you with the procedure. Therefore, continue completing rows of beads until the bracelet is sufficiently length.

Step 4: Complete the Beaded Bracelet on the Loom

Continue weaving rows of beads until the bracelet reaches the desired length. I made two bracelets, the first of which was backed with a shred of suede. I truly like (and prefer) the design of the second bracelet I fashioned, which lacks the backing.

To assure that the bracelet would not unravel, I utilized the technique shown in this book. However, I did not go back and forth as often as this individual. I felt comfortable going back and forth with the thread a few times. I then secured the end with a knot. Then, armed with fabric glue, I liberally coated the thread ends with adhesive. As a result of the knot at the end and the application of glue, it is now quite secure. I let it to air-dry overnight.

The next morning, I pulled everything from the loom and used scissors to trim the superfluous thread. I cut a piece of suede for the bigger bracelet and then attached the beaded piece to it. I then cut out many more suede pieces and put them together. For the second bracelet (my favorite), I ended up adhering the beads and trimmed them in the same manner as before. Then, I decided to cut four little suede rectangles and effectively sandwich the thread's end. Before sandwiching it between the suede layers, I adhered it. Then, I laid the ends beneath the weight of the wooden loom and let it to dry thoroughly. I removed any surplus (see images). Then, I extracted the metal clasps and the multi-tool from my pocket. Using the flat portion of the pliers, I began to gently close the clasp. Then, I slipped it over the suede end cap. Then, I completely attached the clasp to the end piece and removed any leftover material. I was then required to join many loops and a final clasp.

Now the bracelets are complete! The whole procedure, particularly the actual beading, was both enjoyable and soothing. I really liked it and eagerly anticipate my next beaded creation. If time permits, I will publish more short movies that may assist you with the project.

Avoid These Common Beginning Beading Mistakes

If you start out on the proper path, beading can be an enjoyable, soothing, and delightfully creative activity with a wealth of options. To assist you in this endeavor, we have compiled a list of typical beading errors, along with advice on how to prevent them.

Utilizing the Incorrect Beads for a Project

It is tempting to begin a beading project or design with whatever beads you have on hand when you are just beginning. Occasionally this works, but occasionally it may not. The beadwork may not lay flat or retain its intended form, beads may seem to be improperly spaced, or your finished design may not look right and you cannot determine why.

Beadwork on a loom, for instance, will always seem more consistent when completed with Japanese cylinder beads.

Before attributing this to poor skill, investigate if the problem is with your beads. If you use beads that are even slightly different in size, shape, or manufacturer from those specified in a project's directions, your beadwork will vary from the sample. This is due to the fact that tiny changes in bead geometry are amplified by the enormous number of beads in the majority of beadwork. Using bigger beads than specified in the instructions may have a significant effect on the thread tension of the product.

Experience will teach you how to choose suitable alternative beads for the various tasks and designs you meet. In the meanwhile, adhere as closely as possible to the project instructions or make replacements only where the project calls for other kinds of beads.

Beadwork With Excessive Thread

Beginner beaders are most irritated by the prospect of having to stop numerous times throughout a project to add more beading thread.

To prevent this, you might try sewing using a long-lasting, extra-long piece of thread. Unfortunately, the lengthy thread has a number of disadvantages.

First, it can catch on almost anything, from your shoelaces to the edge of your desk. Second, a longer thread is more likely to get tangled than a shorter one. The time spent separating tangles and untying knots may rapidly outweigh the time saved by replacing thread less often.

In the beginning, the extra-long thread increases the amount of effort required for each stitch. To finish a single stitch in beading, you must draw the thread through a bead, pause, pull the thread again, halt, and maybe pull the thread again. When working with a shorter thread, one or two pulls are sufficient for each stitch, resulting in a quicker completion of the job.

The longer thread is susceptible to more wear as it is dragged through the beads, which may lead it to break either during the beading process or after the product has been done.

What is the solution? Begin by drawing an arm's length of thread at a time. And be patient while adding a new thread; you will get used to it over time.

Incorrect Beading Thread Tension

Thread tension impacts the drape of your beading. When tension is too high, beading curls or puckers, and when tension is too low, beadwork is floppy and may seem to have holes.

There's no getting around the reality that proper thread tension requires practice. However, the process may be sped up by forming excellent habits early on. Learn to give the thread a little pull once every stitch has been completed. For applications requiring "tight" tension, you may make that a strong pull.

Also consider how your beadwork handling influences thread tension. You may discover, for instance, that when you halt and lay down your beading, the tension eases. Before you begin sewing again, make careful to give the thread a few pulls to prevent leaving a slack region with gaps between beads.

Although too tight thread tension is permanent, too-loose tension may typically be adjusted.

Separating Beading Thread

Thread splitting happens when your beading needle accidentally passes through the thread in your beaded. It may cause the last bead to twist instead of snapping into place and laying flat. Additionally, split thread causes weak points in your beading and makes it more difficult to rip out an error.

Fortunately, the majority of beads used for beadweaving have big holes that permit many, clean thread passes. Position your needle as far away as possible from the current thread inside each bead to prevent thread splitting.

Fear of Trying New Beadwork Stitches

There are several stitches and methods to master in beadweaving, but not all of them will become your favorites. But avoid creating stitch phobias, in which you avoid a beadweaving stitch because you believe it will be difficult to master.

Peyote stitch with an odd number of threads is feared by many beginners. Some individuals believe that weaving around the beads to reposition the needle will be far more difficult than sewing even-count flat peyote. However, odd-count flat peyote provides design options that would be difficult or impossible to accomplish otherwise, such as centering patterns and creating curved beading. If you avoid this stitch, your inventiveness will be severely constrained.

Select the stitches you want to learn depending on the outcomes they provide. If you appreciate the potential of a stitch, you should explore it. Just be patient and remember that every beadweaving thread is achievable. And with experience, even the most difficult methods will become simpler.

Instead of expecting a beautiful piece of beaded jewelry when you first begin a new stitch, create a practice piece first.

www.ingramcontent.com/pod-product-compliance
Lightning Source LLC
LaVergne TN
LVHW081029181224
799426LV00013B/776